Heroes of Faith:
Powerful Faith-Building Quotes
From Leading Classic Charismatic
Ministers of All Time

Harrison House
Tulsa, Oklahoma

Heroes of Faith: Powerful Faith-Building Quotes
From Leading Classic Charismatic Ministers of All Time
ISBN 0-89274-983-0
Copyright © 1996 by **Harrison House, Inc.**
P. O. Box 35035
Tulsa, Oklahoma 74153

Introduction

Heroes of Faith: Powerful Faith-Building Quotes From Leading Classic Charismatic Ministers of All Time gathers together in one collection life-changing insights from men and women of faith from the past who knew their God and did great and mighty exploits for Him. Their insights, accompanied by the simplicity of God's Word, will speak to you right where you are.

Filled with the power and the Spirit of the Charismatic movement, this little book will stir up in you the God-given gifts and abilities which will enable you to fulfill the purpose for which you were created. Allow Him to speak to your spirit as you read from men and women such as Kathryn Kuhlman, Smith Wigglesworth, William Seymour, Aimee Semple McPherson, A. A. Allen, Maria Woodworth-Etter, Lilian Yeomans, F. F. Bosworth, Gordon Lindsay and many more. Dare to believe God for great and mighty things and go all the way with Him.

There are boundless possibilities
for us if we dare to act in God
and dare to believe.
Smith Wigglesworth

"If I can do anything!" retorted Jesus.
"Everything is possible to the man who believes."
MARK 9:23 PHILLIPS

If you are walking with Jesus, in the Spirit, you need not fear going too far. No believer has gone as far as God wants him to go.

A. A. Allen

Brethren, I count not myself to have apprehended: but this one thing I do, forgetting those things which are behind, and reaching forth unto those things which are before.

PHILIPPIANS 3:13

John Alexander Dowie built the city
of Zion, Illinois, to God . . . . every road
led to the church at the center of town.
As of today, there are still
no bars or clubs in the city.

Real prayer — determined, prevailing prayer — is the greatest outlet of power on earth.

A. A. Allen

Confess your faults one to another, and pray one for another, that ye may be healed. The effectual fervent prayer of a righteous man availeth much.

JAMES 5:16

The only limit to the power of God
lies within the individual.
Kathryn Kuhlman

*Jesus saith unto her, Said I not unto thee, that, if thou
wouldest believe, thou shouldest see the glory of God?*
JOHN 11:40

Kathryn Kuhlman did not experience the supernatural healings in her ministry that she was known for until she gave up everything for the Lord in 1945. She expressed this as "dying to self."

All He [God] asks for is that
simplicity of faith which will
take Him at His Word.
James Salter

Jesus answered, "The work of God is this:
to believe in the one he has sent."
JOHN 6:29 NIV

A person does not become converted by turning over a new leaf or living a better life; He is converted when the power of God gives Him new life.

Howard Carter

There is a new creation whenever a man comes to be in Christ; what is old is gone, the new has come.
2 CORINTHIANS 5:17 MOFFATT

You have within you now all the
elements that are necessary to make
you all that the Father dreamed
that you would be in Christ.

E. W. Kenyon

*Blessed be the God and Father of our
Lord Jesus Christ, who hath blessed us with
all spiritual blessings in heavenly places in Christ.*
EPHESIANS 1:3

Go all the way, don't let anything keep you from appropriating the promises of God in your own life.

A. A. Allen

That ye be not slothful, but followers of them who through faith and patience inherit the promises.
HEBREWS 6:12

God rejoices when we manifest a faith
that holds Him to His Word.
Smith Wigglesworth

*Put Me in remembrance [remind Me of your merits];
let us plead and argue together. Set forth your case,
that you may be justified (proved right).*
ISAIAH 43:26 AMP

Faith must rest on the will of God alone, not on our desires or wishes. Appropriating faith is not believing that God can but that God will.

F. F. Bosworth

And, behold, there came a leper and worshipped him, saying, Lord, if thou wilt, thou canst make me clean.
MATTHEW 8:2

It is when active faith dares to believe God to the point of action, that something has to happen.
Kathryn Kuhlman

Fool! When will you ever learn that "believing" is useless without doing what God wants you to? Faith that does not result in good deeds is not real faith.
JAMES 2:20 TLB

What is the greatest secret of life? Is it not that the Creator has a plan for every person born into the world?
Gordon Lindsay

But in fact God has arranged the parts in the body, every one of them, just as he wanted them to be.
1 CORINTHIANS 12:18 NIV

Salvation is from God and not from man. It was thought by God the Father, bought by the Son, and wrought by the Spirit.

P. C. Nelson

And such were some of you: but ye are washed, but ye are sanctified, but ye are justified in the name of the Lord Jesus, and by the Spirit of our God.

1 Corinthians 6:11

The things of God are so precious, He
will not give them to those who do not
greatly desire them. It is those who
hunger and thirst who are filled.

C. Nuzum

*"Blessed are those who hunger and thirst for
righteousness, for they shall be satisfied."*
MATTHEW 5:6 NAS

There is a reason why some have power and some do not. And it is not because God is a respecter of persons. Favor is a direct result of faith, and faith comes by obedience.

A. A. Allen

So then faith cometh by hearing, and hearing by the word of God.
ROMANS 10:17

The power of the Holy Ghost may be readily likened to the power of electricity. When one is filled with the Spirit, it is as though he has had his house wired, and established connection with the "powerhouse."

A. A. Allen

But ye shall receive power, after that the Holy Ghost is come upon you: and ye shall be witnesses unto me both in Jerusalem, and in all Judaea, and in Samaria, and unto the uttermost part of the earth.

ACTS 1:8

Our bodies are His temples and, as great
pieces of mechanism are moved by electricity,
so our bodies, the most wonderful piece
of mechanism ever known, are moved by
the power of the Holy Ghost.
Maria Woodworth-Etter

*And what union can there be between God's temple and
idols? For you are God's temple, the home of the living God,
and God has said of you, "I will live in them and walk
among them, and I will be their God and they shall
be my people."*

2 CORINTHIANS 6:16 TLB

Dare to stand in the presence of sense knowledge facts, and declare that you are what God says you are.

E. W. Kenyon

"Truly I say to you, whoever says to this mountain, 'Be taken up and cast into the sea,' and does not doubt in his heart, but believes that what he says is going to happen, it shall be granted him."
MARK 11:23 NAS

Jesus can heal anything, anywhere, any time, and anybody. All you have to do is put your faith in Him.

Jack Coe

When the even was come, they brought unto him many that were possessed with devils: and he cast out the spirits with his word, and healed all that were sick.
MATTHEW 8:16

Faith begins where the will
of God is known.
F. F. Bosworth

*We conclude that faith is awakened by
the message, and the message that awakens
it comes through the word of Christ.*
ROMANS 10:17 NEB

Real faith believes God right to the end.
Smith Wigglesworth

*Therefore, do not throw away your confidence,
which has a great reward. For you have need
of endurance, so that when you have done the
will of God, you may receive what was promised.*
HEBREWS 10:35,36 NAS

God's ways are not our ways.
Lillian Trasher

"For My thoughts are not your thoughts,
Neither are your ways My ways," declares the LORD.
ISAIAH 55:8 NAS

It is only the power of God
that can sustain.
Aimee Semple McPherson

Who being the brightness of his glory, and the express image of his person, and upholding all things by the word of his power, when he had by himself purged our sins, sat down on the right hand of the Majesty on high.
Hebrews 1:3

The power of God is equal to every emergency and is great enough for the deliverance of every soul from every oppression.

John G. Lake

And my speech and my preaching was not with enticing words of man's wisdom, but in demonstration of the Spirit and of power: That your faith should not stand in the wisdom of men, but in the power of God.

1 CORINTHIANS 2:4,5

If you are in desperate need of deliverance, do not hesitate to cry to the Lord. He hears those who call upon Him with all their heart.

Gordon Lindsay

*Then shall ye call upon me, and ye shall go and
pray unto me, and I will hearken unto you.
And ye shall seek me, and find me, when
ye shall search for me with all your heart.*
JEREMIAH 29:12,13

Temptation will come, but God will be
with you right in the temptation
to deliver you.
Smith Wigglesworth

*Let your conversation be without covetousness; and be
content with such things as ye have: for he hath said, I
will never leave thee, nor forsake thee.*
HEBREWS 13:5

Remember the will of man is the biggest hinderance to God.
Stanley Frodsham

Then Jesus said to His disciples, If anyone is desiring to come after me, let him forget self and lose sight of his own interests, and let him pick up his cross and carry it.
MATTHEW 16:24 WUEST

Seeing only what God says will produce and increase faith. Don't doubt your faith, doubt your doubts for they are unreliable.

F. F. Bosworth

My son, attend to my words; incline thine ear unto my sayings. Let them not depart from thine eyes; keep them in the midst of thine heart. For they are life unto those that find them, and health to all their flesh.

PROVERBS 4:20,22

The devil is busy trying to take from us
what we take from God, and so God
bids us hold fast.

C. Nuzum

*Let us hold fast the confession of the hope without
wavering (for faithful is He Who promised).*
HEBREWS 10:23 WORRELL

Finis Jennings Dake spent forty-three years researching and writing the annotations for the *Dake's Annotated Reference Bible.*

Loss of communion is the explanation of most of our failure in spiritual fruitbearing.

Donald Gee

If we say that we have fellowship with Him and yet walk in the darkness, we lie and do not practice the truth.
1 JOHN 1:6 NAS

You get faith by studying the Word.
Study that Word until something in you
"knows that you know" and that you do
not just hope that you know.
Carrie Judd Montgomery

*That is why I am suffering as I am. Yet I am not
ashamed, because I know whom I have believed, and am
convinced that he is able to guard what I have entrusted to
him for that day.*
2 TIMOTHY 1:12 NIV

When God talks to you, the message agrees with the written Word; the Holy Ghost never says anything that doesn't correspond with the Word.

Maria Woodworth-Etter

For there are three that bear record in heaven, the Father, the Word, and the Holy Ghost: and these three are one.
1 JOHN 5:7

Ignorance will rob us of what we could otherwise possess and use.

Howard Carter

My people are destroyed from lack of knowledge. "Because you have rejected knowledge, I also reject you as my priests; because you have ignored the law of your God, I also will ignore your children."

HOSEA 4:6 NIV

Appropriating faith cannot go beyond
our knowledge of the revealed
will of God.

F. F. Bosworth

*So then faith cometh by hearing,
and hearing by the word of God.*
ROMANS 10:17

A spiritual law that few recognize is that our confession rules us. It is what we confess with our lips that really dominates our inner being.

F. F. Bosworth

But we have the same Spirit of faith [as the Psalmist] according as it has been written and is at present on record, I believed, wherefore I spoke.
2 CORINTHIANS 4:13 WUEST

Just believe what God says that Jesus
has done for you, body, soul, and spirit
— think about it, talk about it,
sing about it, shout about it,
and the praise cure has begun.

Lilian B. Yeomans

*Therefore I say unto you, What things soever ye desire,
when ye pray, believe that ye receive them,
and ye shall have them.*

MARK 11:24

If you've got just a little bit of faith as a grain
of mustard seed, and begin to praise God,
that faith will mount up, until fear
won't be able to stay in your heart.

Jack Coe

*And Jesus said unto them, Because of your unbelief: for
verily I say unto you, If ye have faith as a grain of
mustard seed, ye shall say unto this mountain, Remove
hence to yonder place; and it shall remove; and nothing
shall be impossible unto you.*

MATTHEW 17:20

Evan Roberts in 1904 led a great outpouring of the Holy Spirit in Wales called the Welsh Revival. He was known for never taking any credit but giving God all the glory.

God wants us of one accord; hearts
running together like drops of water.
Maria Woodworth-Etter

*Fill up and complete my joy by living in harmony and
being of the same mind and one in purpose, having the
same love, being in full accord and of one harmonious
mind and intention.*
Philippians 2:2 AMP

Every thought of advantage for ourselves must be on the decrease in order that Christ may increase.
Smith Wigglesworth

He must increase, but I must decrease.
JOHN 3:30

Fear cannot stay in the same house
with Jesus Christ.
Jack Coe

*For God did not give us a spirit of timidity,
but a spirit of power, of love and of self-discipline.*
2 TIMOTHY 1:7 NIV

God is a good God.
James Salter

*O give thanks to the Lord, for He is good; for His mercy
and loving-kindness endure forever!*
PSALM 107:1 AMP

God's promises work their wonders
while we see and act on eternal realities
and refuse to be affected by temporal
things to the contrary.

F. F. Bosworth

*While we look not at the things which are seen, but at the
things which are not seen: for the things which are seen
are temporal; but the things which are not seen are eternal.*
2 CORINTHIANS 4:18

There must be a holding in subjection of the whole being. The body must be the servant, never once the master.

John Alexander Dowie

No, I maul and master my body, lest, after preaching to other people, I am disqualified myself.
1 CORINTHIANS 9:27 MOFFATT

God does not patch up the old life, or make certain repairs on the old life; He gives a new life, through the new birth.

Kathryn Kuhlman

Therefore if any man be in Christ, he is a new creature: old things are passed away; behold, all things are become new.

2 CORINTHIANS 5:17

In me is working a power stronger than every other power. The life that is in me is a thousand times bigger than I am outside.

Smith Wigglesworth

I have been crucified with Christ and I no longer live, but Christ lives in me. The life I live in the body, I live by faith in the Son of God, who loved me and gave himself for me.

GALATIANS 2:20 NIV

My righteousness is just as good as
Jesus' righteousness because
it is Jesus' righteousness.

E. W. Kenyon

*But of him are ye in Christ Jesus, who of God is made
unto us wisdom, and righteousness, and sanctification,
and redemption.*

1 CORINTHIANS 1:30

Without the Spirit's aid we cannot live
as we should or do what we ought.
P. C. Nelson

*"And I will ask the Father, and He will give you another
Helper, that He may be with you forever."*
JOHN 14:16 NAS

There are many Christians who are Christians in theory only, and they are worldlings in practice.

John Alexander Dowie

For as the body without the spirit is dead, so faith without works is dead also.
JAMES 2:26

Justification is what God
does for us, while sanctification
is what God does in us.
P. C. Nelson

*But of Him are ye in Christ Jesus,
Who was made to us wisdom from God, also
righteousness, and holiness, and redemption.*
1 CORINTHIANS 1:30 WORRELL

Anyone who has faith to comply with
the commission James gives can pray
the prayer of faith for the sick and
they will be healed.

Maria Woodworth-Etter

*Is any sick among you? let him call for the elders
of the church; and let them pray over him, anointing
him with oil in the name of the Lord.*

JAMES 5:14

It is not faith in God's power that
secures His blessings but faith
in His love and in His will.

F. F. Bosworth

*God is, as to His nature, love, and he who
dwells in the aforementioned love in God is dwelling,
and God in him is dwelling.*
1 JOHN 4:16 WUEST

God supplies the miracle of the new birth experience — He supplies the power — Jesus supplies the pardon, but we must supply the willingness.

Kathryn Kuhlman

Being born again, not of corruptible seed, but of incorruptible, by the word of God, which liveth and abideth for ever.

1 PETER 1:23

If any man wills to be a Christian,
he can be a Christian. If you go to hell,
you go of your own accord.
Aimee Semple McPherson

*For this is good and acceptable in the sight of God our
Saviour; Who will have all men to be saved, and to come
unto the knowledge of the truth.*
1 TIMOTHY 2:3,4

Maria Woodworth-Etter recorded
incidents of speaking in tongues
as early as 1895.

Jesus Christ dwells in us.
We are God's powerhouse.
Maria Woodworth-Etter

*With Christ I have been crucified, and it is no longer
I who live, but there lives in me Christ. And that
life which now I live in the sphere of the flesh,
by faith I live it, which faith is in the Son of God
who loved me and gave himself on my behalf.*
GALATIANS 2:20 WUEST

God cannot declare one not guilty
before He is cleansed from all sin and
made holy by the blood of Christ.

Finis Jennings Dake

*If we confess our sins, He is faithful and righteous
to forgive us our sins and to cleanse us from
all unrighteousness.*

1 JOHN 1:9 NAS

There is a place for us in Christ Jesus
where we are no longer under
condemnation but where the
heavens are always open to us.

Smith Wigglesworth

For the eyes of the Lord are over the righteous,
and his ears are open unto their prayers:
but the face of the Lord is against them that do evil.
1 PETER 3:12

Exercise the spirit of faith
as much as you do the act of prayer.
Be humble and watchfully obedient,
that faith be not clouded.
Raymond T. Richey

*But since our spirit of faith is the same, therefore —
as it is written I believed and so I spoke.*
2 CORINTHIANS 4:13 MOFFATT

Children of God, who think you
are something, you are nothing;
when you realize you are nothing,
God fights for you.
Maria Woodworth-Etter

*Ye shall not need to fight in this battle: set yourselves,
stand ye still, and see the salvation of the LORD with you, O
Judah and Jerusalem: fear not, nor be dismayed; to morrow
go out against them: for the LORD will be with you.*
2 CHRONICLES 20:17

We are not to be occupied with
our feelings or symptoms or our faith,
or lack of faith, but only with
what God has said.

Gordon Lindsay

*Who against hope believed in hope, that he might
become the father of many nations, according
to that which was spoken, So shall thy seed be.*

ROMANS 4:18

When we pick up the Bible it would be good to remember that It is the Book with God in It; life in It; a God-indwelt Book.

E. W. Kenyon

In the beginning the Word was existing.
And the Word was in fellowship with God the Father.
And the Word was as to His essence absolute deity.
JOHN 1:1 WUEST

After being sufficiently enlightened,
our attitude toward sickness should be
the same as our attitude toward sin.

F. F. Bosworth

*Who his own self bare our sins in his own body on the
tree, that we, being dead to sins, should live unto
righteousness: by whose stripes ye were healed.*
1 PETER 2:24

Raymond T. Richey led some of the greatest healing meetings that Tulsa, Oklahoma, has ever seen. There were so many healings that large trucks were loaded down with crutches and wheelchairs once the meeting was over.

Christ is seeking the affection
of mankind, the union of their
spirit with His.
John G. Lake

*We want you to be with us in this – in this fellowship
with the Father, and Jesus Christ his Son.*
1 JOHN 1:3 PHILLIPS

Before one can walk as Christ walked,
and talk as He talked, he must first
begin to think as Christ thought.
A. A. Allen

Let this mind be in you, which was also in Christ Jesus.
PHILIPPIANS 2:5

William J. Seymour began the Azusa Street revival in an abandoned church after he had been asked to step down as the associate pastor of a holiness church due to doctrinal differences. Today many Pentecostal groups can trace their lineage to this revival.

The Holy Spirit came to give us power
to stand on the infallible Word
and overcome false spirits.
William Seymour

Ye are of God, little children, and have overcome them:
because greater is he that is in you,
than he that is in the world.
1 JOHN 4:4

A man that preaches like a saint in his church, and lives like a devil in his home is one of the worst of men.

John Alexander Dowie

So speak, and so do, as those who are about to be judged by a law of liberty.
JAMES 2:12 WORRELL

But if we are to be like Him [Jesus]
in power, we must also be like Him in
holiness, in consecration, in meekness,
and in compassion.

A. A. Allen

*The disciple is not above his master: but every
one that is perfect shall be as his master.*
LUKE 6:40

The great mystery hid in God in all past ages was that of making Jews and Gentiles one new Body — the Church, which is His Body.
Finis Jennings Dake

By his death he ended the angry resentment between us, caused by the Jewish laws which favored the Jews and excluded the Gentiles, for he died to annul that whole system of Jewish laws. Then he took the two groups that had been opposed to each other and made them parts of himself; thus he fused us together to become one new person, and at last there was peace.
EPHESIANS 2:15 TLB

The Church consists of people who have been "called out of" sin and the world and who have assembled for a common purpose.

P. C. Nelson

*Wherefore come out from among them,
and be ye separate, saith the Lord, and touch
not the unclean thing; and I will receive you.*
2 CORINTHIANS 6:17

Your spirit life is fortified and built up
and enriched by communion with the
Father and by reading His Word.
John G. Lake

He that speaketh in an unknown tongue edifieth himself;
but he that prophesieth edifieth the church.
1 CORINTHIANS 14:4

Spiritual fruit is the outcome
of the life of unbroken and full
communion with Christ.
Donald Gee

*I am the vine itself, you are the branches. It is the man
who shares my life and whose life I share who proves
fruitful. For apart from me you can do nothing at all.*
JOHN 15:5 PHILLIPS

Man is God-hungry.
Jesus is the solution of the problem.
Through Jesus Christ we become
partakers of the divine nature.
John G. Lake

The thief cometh not, but for to steal, and to kill, and to destroy: I am come that they might have life, and that they might have it more abundantly.

John 10:10

The fruit of the Spirit is the direct result
of the life of Christ ministered to the
believer by the Spirit.
Donald Gee

*But the fruit of the Spirit is love, joy, peace,
long-suffering, kindness, goodness, faith, meekness,
continence; against such there is no law.*
GALATIANS 5:22 WORRELL

Prayer and prayer alone, much prayer, persistent prayer, is the door of entrance into the heart of God.

John G. Lake

Now He was telling them a parable to show that at all times they ought to pray and not to lose heart.
LUKE 18:1 NAS

A life of holiness is essential to a life of physical wholeness; and both are ours through faith in the Lamb of God.

Lilian B. Yeomans

Having therefore these promises, dearly beloved, let us cleanse ourselves from all filthiness of the flesh and spirit, perfecting holiness in the fear of God.

2 CORINTHIANS 7:1

The validity of the Christian faith rests on one supreme miracle — the resurrection of Jesus Christ.

Kathryn Kuhlman

That if thou shalt confess with thy mouth the Lord Jesus, and shalt believe in thine heart that God hath raised him from the dead, thou shalt be saved.

ROMANS 10:9

Christ is more than the foundation of the Church. He is the rock on which the foundation is founded.
John Alexander Dowie

They all ate the same supernatural food, and all drank the same supernatural drink; I mean, they all drank from the supernatural rock that accompanied their travels — and that rock was Christ.
1 CORINTHIANS 10:3,4 NEB

In order for a church to prosper, she
must obey Jesus' teaching in all things.
William Seymour

*If you will only let me help you, if you will only obey,
then I will make you rich!*
ISAIAH 1:19 TLB

Every believer has a vital function
in the church, even though it may
seem insignificant.
P. C. Nelson

*No, much rather, the members of the body
which seem to be more feeble, are necessary.*
1 CORINTHIANS 12:22 WUEST

You have just as much right to step
into the presence of God Almighty
as Jesus has.
John G. Lake

For he hath made him to be sin for us, who knew no sin;
that we might be made the righteousness of God in him.
2 CORINTHIANS 5:21

Fellowship in its fulness is the soil out of which living faith grows to fruition.

E. W. Kenyon

It is of what we saw and heard that we bring you word, so that you may share our fellowship; and our fellowship is with the Father and with his Son Jesus Christ.

1 JOHN 1:3 MOFFATT

If you have worry, you don't have faith,
and if you have faith,
you don't have worry.

Jack Coe

And he saith unto them, Why are ye fearful,
O ye of little faith? Then he arose, and rebuked
the winds and the sea; and there was a great calm.
Matthew 8:26

To commit suggests not only
bringing the matter to God,
but also leaving it there.
Gordon Lindsay

*Commit your way to the LORD, Trust also in Him,
and He will do it.*
PSALM 37:5 NAS

We must ever abide under the shadow of the cross, and the result will be perfect physical, as well as spiritual, victory.

Lilian B. Yeomans

Blotting out the handwriting of ordinances that was against us, which was contrary to us, and took it out of the way, nailing it to his cross; And having spoiled principalities and powers, he made a shew of them openly, triumphing over them in it.

Colossians 2:14,15

Lift up your heads, ye people,
lift up your faces, too, open your
mouths to sing His praise,
and the rain will fall on you.
Aimee Semple McPherson

*My whole being shall be satisfied as with marrow and
fatness; and my mouth shall praise You with joyful lips.*
PSALM 63:5 AMP

If regeneration has to do with our nature, justification with our standing, and adoption with our position, then sanctification has to do with our character and conduct.

P. C. Nelson

For this is the will of God, even your sanctification, that ye should abstain from fornication.
1 THESSALONIANS 4:3

Call it what you will — perfection, holiness, entire sanctification — it is not only possible, it is not only our privilege, it is God's command.

A. A. Allen

Follow peace with all men, and holiness, without which no man shall see the Lord.
HEBREWS 12:14

Because Christ lives, our faith is not vain —
our preaching is not vain; and wonder of
wonders is that this exceeding greatness of
power is at our disposal.

Kathryn Kuhlman

*And what is the exceeding greatness of his power
to usward who believe, according to the working
of his mighty power, Which he wrought in Christ,
when he raised him from the dead, and set him
at his own right hand in the heavenly places.*

EPHESIANS 1:19,20

The Lord Jesus Christ left us a legacy,
He has left us gifts of the Holy Ghost,
and concerning these spiritual gifts we
ought not to be ignorant.

Howard Carter

*Now about the spiritual gifts (the special endowments
of supernatural energy), brethren, I do not
want you to be misinformed.*
1 CORINTHIANS 12:1 AMP

The anointing of the Holy Spirit is given to illuminate His Word, to open the Scriptures, and to place the spiritual man in direct communication with the mind of God.

Charles F. Parham

And the Anointing which ye received from Him abideth in you, and ye have no need that anyone teach you; but as His Anointing teacheth you concerning all things, and is true, and is no lie, and even as He taught you, ye abide in Him.

1 JOHN 2:27 WORRELL

Charles Parham was known to have taught about the Holy Spirit at his Bible school in Topeka, Kansas ... here is one of the first recordings of speaking in tongues in the early 1900s.

Be God's stewards and give the Lord
His part. He gives you everything you have,
physical, financial and spiritual; and He
expects you to use all your powers for Him.
Maria Woodworth-Etter

*God that made the world and all things therein, seeing
that he is Lord of heaven and earth, dwelleth not in
temples made with hands; Neither is worshipped with
men's hands, as though he needed any thing, seeing he
giveth to all life, and breath, and all things.*
Acts 17:24,25

He who proves God will find that the very
windows of heaven will open
and a blessing will come down
greater than he is able to receive.
Gordon Lindsay

*Bring ye all the tithes into the storehouse, that there may
be meat in mine house, and prove me now herewith, saith
the LORD of hosts, if I will not open you the windows
of heaven, and pour you out a blessing, that there shall
not be room enough to receive it.*
MALACHI 3:10

God does not give His gifts to be played
with, when they are not required.
But they are active and ready when
the need arises, for those who will
put their trust in Him.
Gordon Lindsay

*God also testified to it by signs,
wonders and various miracles, and gifts of
the Holy Spirit distributed according to his will.*
HEBREWS 2:4 NIV

Faith is the hand with which we take from God. When we have met all the conditions and taken what God is offering us, we must believe that we have that thing.

C. Nuzum

Therefore I say unto you, What things soever ye desire, when ye pray, believe that ye receive them, and ye shall have them.

MARK 11:24

Gordon Lindsay is the founder of Christ for the Nations Bible School in Waxahachie, Texas.

God gives us an opportunity to act our faith. When we give larger as an act of our faith in God's promise, we show confidence that God will not fail us.

Gordon Lindsay

But this I say, He which soweth sparingly shall reap also sparingly; and he which soweth bountifully shall reap also bountifully.
2 CORINTHIANS 9:6

It is the foursquare gospel from the foursquare city with a foursquare message to bring — Jesus only Saviour, Baptizer and Healer;
Jesus the coming King.
Aimee Semple McPherson

For I resolved to know nothing while I was with you except Jesus Christ and him crucified.
1 CORINTHIANS 2:2 NIV

A God Who understands; a God Who knows
our every weakness, our every failure,
our every shortcoming, our every sin —
and yet He continues to love us and
to pour His mercy upon us.

Kathryn Kuhlman

*But after that the kindness and love of God our Saviour toward
man appeared, Not by works of righteousness which we have
done, but according to his mercy he saved us, by the washing
of regeneration, and renewing of the Holy Ghost.*

Titus 3:4,5

God's name is, "I am that I am." He is the Almighty; He is omnipotent; He is omniscient. He brings the eternal past and the eternal future into the present.

Howard Carter

God said to Moses, "I AM WHO I AM. This is what you are to say to the Israelites: 'I AM has sent me to you.'"
EXODUS 3:14 NIV

Maria Woodworth-Etter once stood in a trance in one of her meetings for three days with her hand in the air! Many people in her meetings experienced trances in which they had glimpses of heaven.

You do not base your belief that Jesus is the Saviour from sin upon the fact that somebody is saved, or says he is saved; but you base it upon the Word of the living God; and there you stand.

John Alexander Dowie

But what does it say? The Word (God's message in Christ) is near you, on your lips and in your heart; that is, the Word (the message, the basis and object) of faith which we preach.

ROMANS 10:8 AMP

Self-effacement and repentance,
acceptance of extended mercies, and
unwavering dependence on God's
promises is the only highway
to genuine spiritual exultation.
Charles F. Parham

*Let us hold fast the profession of our faith without
wavering; (for he is faithful that promised).*
HEBREWS 10:23

In becoming part of the Body of Christ,
sickness should have no more mastery
over us than it had over the Body of
Christ when He was on earth.

Gordon Lindsay

For we are members of his body,
of his flesh, and of his bones.
EPHESIANS 5:30

When Smith Wigglesworth's beloved
wife died, he prayed for her to be raised
from the dead. She came back to life
but told her husband that she wanted
to go home. He then kissed her, and
she went on to be with the Lord.

With God all things are possible, and all things are possible to him who believeth, for faith makes room for God to work and thus releases omnipotence.

Lilian B. Yeomans

"'If you can'?" said Jesus.
"Everything is possible for him who believes."
MARK 9:23 NIV

He is omnipotent, omnipresent
and omniscient; therefore, He is not limited
by time nor is He limited by man's ideologies,
theologies, and preconceived ideas.
Kathryn Kuhlman

*Remember the former things of old: for I am God, and
there is none else; I am God, and there is none like me,
Declaring the end from the beginning, and from ancient
times the things that are not yet done, saying, My counsel
shall stand, and I will do all my pleasure.*
ISAIAH 46:9,10

The measure of the stature of the fullness is seldom mentioned, much less demonstrated, while the stature of littleness, emptiness, and powerlessness of Christianity is often emphasized and demonstrated.

Finis Jennings Dake

Until we all attain to the unity of the faith, and of the full knowledge of the Son of God, to a full-grown man — to the measure of the stature of the fulness of Christ.

EPHESIANS 4:13 WORRELL

No Christian should make excuses for his own imperfections, but should recognize them as failures to keep the command of Christ, and strive earnestly to overcome them. Perfection is the goal.

A. A. Allen

Be ye therefore perfect, even as your Father which is in heaven is perfect.

MATTHEW 5:48

If you want a simple word to characterize the person of God, all you will have to do is to take four letters and write them over and over again — the word, *love* — and that's God.

Kathryn Kuhlman

And we have known and believed the love that God hath to us. God is love; and he that dwelleth in love dwelleth in God, and God in him.

1 JOHN 4:16

As soon as you know your sins are forgiven, be sure that you make your "back-tracks" as clean and straight as possible . . . get the love of God into your heart . . . love that can love even your brother-in-law.

Aimee Semple McPherson

As for us, we know absolutely that we have passed over permanently out of the death into the life, because we are habitually loving the brethren with a divine and self-sacrificial love.

1 JOHN 3:14 WUEST

The farther we get in God the hotter
the fire will be because the
infinitesimal dross requires a
hotter fire to get it out of the gold.
Charles F. Parham

*These have come so that your faith — of greater worth
than gold, which perishes even though refined by fire —
may be proved genuine and may result in praise, glory
and honor when Jesus Christ is revealed.*
1 PETER 1:7 NIV

Always resist even the appearance of evil. In doing so, evil will never subdue you. The blood of Jesus is the answer.

Lam Jeevarat-Nam

Abstain from all appearance of evil.
1 THESSALONIANS 5:22

There is no disease in God and there is none in heaven. Disease and health cannot come from the same source.

John Alexander Dowie

How God anointed Jesus of Nazareth with the Holy Ghost and with power: who went about doing good, and healing all that were oppressed of the devil; for God was with him.
Acts 10:38

God means for you to be in a place of overcoming, and has put a force within you whereby you may defeat the devil.

Smith Wigglesworth

Ye are of God, little children, and have overcome them; because greater is He Who is in you, than he that is in the world.

1 JOHN 4:4 WORRELL

John G. Lake opened up healing rooms in Spokane, Washington. In five years, more than 100,000 documented healings occurred in his ministry.

Lillian Trasher was a woman of incredible faith who began an orphanage in Egypt that now houses and feeds more than five hundred children and widows on a twelve acre campus.

God delights to heal His people.
God can keep us all well.
Howard Carter

*In his own person he carried our sins to the gibbet, so that
we might cease to live for sin and begin to live for
righteousness. By his wounds you have been healed.*
1 PETER 2:24 NEB

Christ's redeeming work extends to the entire being: body, soul, and spirit.

John Alexander Dowie

And the very God of peace sanctify you wholly; and I pray God your whole spirit and soul and body be preserved blameless unto the coming of our Lord Jesus Christ.

1 THESSALONIANS 5:23

Let no one pray for a mighty baptism of power who is not prepared for deep heart searchings and confession of sin.

Evan Roberts

And, behold, I send the promise of my Father upon you: but tarry ye in the city of Jerusalem, until ye be endued with power from on high.
LUKE 24:49

God's power is the greatest,
and is the only power that will
bring peace to your soul.
Maria Woodworth-Etter

*Now may the God of hope fill you with all joy
and peace in believing, that you may abound
in hope by the power of the Holy Spirit.*
ROMANS 15:13 NAS

God's way of saving the soul, of healing
the body, and of doing everything else
He wants to do, is to send His Word —
His promise — and then keep the
promise whenever it produces faith.

F. F. Bosworth

He sends forth His word and heals them
and rescues them from the pit and destruction.
PSALM 107:20 AMP

Faith is a product of your spirit, not of your intellect. Your intellect does not produce faith. Your knowledge may give you ground for faith, but faith is resident in your spirit.

John G. Lake

For with the heart man believeth unto righteousness; and with the mouth confession is made unto salvation.
ROMANS 10:10

We are conscious of the need of constant prayer for more and yet more of the Holy Spirit's presence and power. But as we give ourselves yet more and more to prayer, we shall see greater and more glorious revivals.
Stanley Frodsham

Ask the LORD for rain in the springtime; it is the LORD who makes the storm clouds. He gives showers of rain to men, and plants of the field to everyone.
ZECHARIAH 10:1 NIV

If you're opposed to divine healing,
you're opposed to the work of the living
God Who's healing scores of souls today —
Who's opening the eyes of the blind, and
causing the lame to walk, and the deaf to hear.

Jack Coe

*And great multitudes came unto him, having with them
those that were lame, blind, dumb, maimed, and many others,
and cast them down at Jesus' feet; and he healed them.*

MATTHEW 15:30

Live in such a way as to pass something tangible to a new generation.
Lillian Trasher

*Whatever you have learned or received or heard
from me, or seen in me — put it into practice.
And the God of peace will be with you.*
PHILIPPIANS 4:9 NIV

Every child of God should have power
enough to bring down a blessing.
There must be faith and obedience.
Maria Woodworth-Etter

*And if we know that he hear us, whatsoever we ask, we
know that we have the petitions that we desired of him.*
1 JOHN 5:15

As you are faithful this one thing is certain, the Lord will show you great and mighty things that you know not now.
Stanley Frodsham

Call to Me and I will answer you and show you great and mighty things, fenced in and hidden, which you do not know (do not distinguish and recognize, have knowledge of and understand).
JEREMIAH 33:3 AMP

When God calls you out for His work, He will take care of you, give you something to eat and clothe you.
Maria Woodworth-Etter

Therefore take no thought, saying, What shall we eat? or, What shall we drink? or, Wherewithal shall we be clothed? (For after all these things do the Gentiles seek:) for your heavenly Father knoweth that ye have need of all these things.
MATTHEW 6:31,32

There is no faith so mighty as passive faith, for strength comes to him that rests in God alone.

John Alexander Dowie

Let us labour therefore to enter into that rest, lest any man fall after the same example of unbelief.

Hebrews 4:11

Never dig up in unbelief
what you have sown in faith.
Gordon Lindsay

But, in view of the promise of God, he wavered not through
unbelief, but was made strong in faith, giving glory to God.
Romans 4:20 Worrell

Many pray about their needs and keep
on praying as though they did not
believe, and in consequence pray
themselves out of faith.

Gordon Lindsay

See to it, brothers, that no one among you has the wicked,
faithless heart of a deserter from the living God.
HEBREWS 3:12 NEB

Rest firmly on the intercession of Jesus Christ. Humbly depend upon the aid of the Holy Spirit.
Raymond T. Richey

Wherefore he is able also to save them to the uttermost that come unto God by him, seeing he ever liveth to make intercession for them.
HEBREWS 7:25

When you have faith in God,
worry has to take its flight.

Jack Coe

*Be careful for nothing; but in every thing by prayer
and supplication with thanksgiving let your
requests be made known unto God.*

PHILIPPIANS 4:6

Trust God, everything will be all right.
Face life with a heart of trust.
Lillian Hunt

*In this confidence let us hold on to the hope
that we profess without the slightest hesitation —
for he is utterly dependable.*
HEBREWS 10:23 PHILLIPS

The purpose of all Scripture is to move us on to this wonderful and blessed elevation of faith where our constant experience is the manifestation of God's life and power through us.
Smith Wigglesworth

For I am not ashamed of the Gospel. It is the saving power of God for everyone who has faith — the Jew first, but the Greek also.
ROMANS 1:16 NEB

The reason people do not have rich, beautiful faith is because their spirit is denied the privilege of communion and fellowship with the Father.
John G. Lake

For the which cause I also suffer these things: nevertheless I am not ashamed: for I know whom I have believed, and am persuaded that he is able to keep that which I have committed unto him against that day.
2 TIMOTHY 1:12

God is the God of the people who are at their wit's end, who are right up against it with their backs to the wall, and He delights to come to our help when we need Him most.

James Salter

I have been young, and now am old; yet have I not seen the righteous forsaken, nor his seed begging bread.

PSALM 37:25

As we unflinchingly take our stand on the naked promise, there springs up within us the "faith of God" which makes walking on the water a delight.
Lilian B. Yeomans

So we fix our eyes not on what is seen, but on what is unseen. For what is seen is temporary, but what is unseen is eternal.
2 Corinthians 4:18 NIV

Aimee Semple McPherson founded the International Church of the Foursquare Gospel in Los Angeles and was known for her dramatic illustrated sermons. Once she even rode into the church on a motorcycle.

It is not what God can do, but what
we know He yearns to do,
that inspires faith.
F. F. Bosworth

*So faith comes from hearing, and hearing
by the word of Christ.*
ROMANS 10:17 NAS

Remember that your thoughts are heard
aloud in heaven. Cultivate the habit
of governing the thoughts and
imaginations. Do not suffer
them to wander.
Raymond T. Richey

*We are destroying speculations and every lofty thing
raised up against the knowledge of God, and we are
taking every thought captive to the obedience of Christ.*
2 CORINTHIANS 10:5 NAS

The success of your life as a child of God will be in exact accordance with the consciousness of the Christ and the power of God that is in your heart.

John G. Lake

I have been crucified with Christ; and no longer am I living, but Christ is living in me; and, in so far as I am now living in flesh, I live in the faith of the Son of God, Who loved me, and gave Himself for me.

GALATIANS 2:20 WORRELL

Endeavor always to remember that you are in the immediate presence of God, and strive to act as you would if you saw the Saviour standing by your side.

Raymond T. Richey

Neither is there any creature that is not manifest in his sight: but all things are naked and opened unto the eyes of him with whom we have to do.

HEBREWS 4:13

Christ within us can accomplish what
we can never hope to do in our own
strength; and that continuous walking
with Him will change the weakest
of us into His image.
Donald Gee

*For in this hope we were saved. But hope that is seen is no
hope at all. Who hopes for what he already has?*
ROMANS 8:24 NIV

God has a realm of divine life opening up to us where there are boundless possibilities, where there is limitless power, where there are untold resources, where we have victory over all the power of the devil.
Smith Wigglesworth

Blessed be the God and Father of our Lord Jesus Christ, who hath blessed us with all spiritual blessings in heavenly places in Christ.
EPHESIANS 1:3

The secret of Christianity is the secret of Christ possessing the heart of man; man being yielded to Him so that His victory, His consciousness, and His power possess your spirit and mind.

John G. Lake

To them God has chosen to make known among the Gentiles the glorious riches of this mystery, which is Christ in you, the hope of glory.

COLOSSIANS 1:27 NIV

Bible References

Unless otherwise indicated, all Scripture quotations are taken from the *King James Version* of the Bible.

Scripture quotations marked (NIV) are taken from the *Holy Bible, New International Version*®. NIV®. Copyright © 1973, 1978, 1984 by International Bible Society. Used by permission of Zondervan Publishing House. All rights reserved.

Scripture quotations marked (AMP) are taken from The Amplified Bible. Old Testament copyright © 1965, 1987 by Zondervan Corporation, Grand Rapids, Michigan. New Testament copyright © 1958, 1987 by the Lockman Foundation, La Habra, California. Used by permission.

Verses marked (TLB) are taken from *The Living Bible* © 1971. Used by permission of Tyndale House Publishers, Inc., Wheaton, Illinois 60189. All rights reserved.

Scripture quotations marked (NEB) are taken from *The New English Bible*. Copyright © The Delegates of the Oxford University Press and the Syndics of the Cambridge University Press 1961, 1970. Reprinted by permission.

The Harrison House Vision

Proclaiming the truth and the power
Of the Gospel of Jesus Christ
With excellence;

Challenging Christians to
Live victoriously,
Grow spiritually,
Know God intimately.